The Jou

Other titles by Avril Rowlands

All the Tales From the Ark

The Animals' Caravan: The Journey Begins
The Animals' Caravan: Stories Jesus Told

Look out for this symbol *. You will find these stories
in the two earlier books of the series.

The Animals' Caravan

The
Journey
continues

Adventures through the Bible
with Caravan Bear and friends

Avril Rowlands

Illustrated by Kay Widdowson

LI🐻N
CHILDREN'S

To Dormouse
With my love and happy memories of adventure in our own caravan,
and to Nick Wright
With my love and thanks for your friendship and help.   A. R.

Text copyright © 2019 Avril Rowlands
Illustrations copyright © 2019 Kay Widdowson
This edition copyright © 2019 Lion Hudson IP Limited

The right of Avril Rowlands to be identified as the author and of Kay
Widdowson to be identified as the illustrator of this work has been asserted by
them in accordance with the Copyright, Designs and Patents Act 1988.

Published by
Lion Hudson Limited
Wilkinson House, Jordan Hill Business Park,
Banbury Road, Oxford OX2 8DR, England
www.lionhudson.com

ISBN 978 0 7459 7811 6
e-ISBN 978 0 7459 7812 3

First edition 2019

A catalogue record for this book is available from the British Library

Printed and bound in the UK, April 2019, LH26

Contents

The Grumbling Israelites

Hector the horse sighed, then snorted loudly as he saw Caravan Bear stagger out of the house laden with pots, pans, and a lot of food.

"We're only going on holiday, not moving home," Hector grumbled as Caravan Bear climbed up the steps and disappeared into the freshly painted bright-red caravan.

There was the sound of banging and thumping as Caravan Bear stowed everything away. He came out holding a long list in his paw.

"We don't want to have to come back because we've forgotten something," he worried.

Just then the back door of the house flew open and Whitby the dog ran out, dragging a box of toys behind her.

"Not more toys!" groaned Hector.

"I don't want to be bored," Whitby explained.

She went back into the house and came out with a large dog basket and piles of cushions.

"There's no room for that basket," Caravan Bear said firmly.

"Oh yes, there is," Whitby barked.

"But I've already put a dog basket in the caravan."

"That one isn't as comfortable as this."

"You didn't seem to mind it last year."

"I've grown since then," Whitby replied. "And I *did* mind it. I just didn't complain."

Hector watched gloomily as Caravan Bear and Whitby packed more and more into the caravan.

"I hope you realize I've got to pull it," he said angrily. "Why do you need all that stuff anyway?"

"We don't, but we might," Caravan Bear retorted, crossing off the items on his list. "We're going away for a long time."

"Wasn't this meant to be a holiday?" Hector muttered.

"It is," said Whitby brightly.

"All I need is a bag full of oats, and that's just to keep up my strength in order to tow this heavy caravan," Hector snorted.

"Oh, stop moaning!" Whitby said before rushing back to the house muttering, "Mustn't forget my toy mice!"

"We're very late," worried Caravan Bear. "Christopher Rabbit will be wondering where we've got to."

Christopher Rabbit *was* wondering where his friends had got to. He had packed his small bag the night before and put it and his Bible in the hall ready for when the caravan arrived. He didn't want to keep them waiting.

For the sixth time, he opened his front door and looked up and down the street. For the sixth time, he consulted the large watch that his grandfather had left him and which kept excellent time.

They were late.

They were very late.

"Perhaps they've forgotten all about me," he thought, as he opened the front door once again.

"Perhaps they've decided to go off without me," he thought as he paced up and down the hall. After all, Caravan Bear, Whitby, and Hector had been friends for a very long time. He had only joined them last year when they set off on their first caravan holiday. That was when Hector had nearly run him down, he remembered with a smile.*

He went into the garden. "Perhaps they don't want me," he thought miserably.

He looked at his watch. They wouldn't come now.

He went back inside and closed his front door. Sadly he picked up his Bible, replaced it on the bookshelf in his living room, and then went to collect his bag.

"Clip clop, clip clop!"

Christopher Rabbit ran to open the door. Racing down the street toward him was Hector, pulling the familiar red caravan with bright yellow wheels. Caravan Bear and Whitby sat on the top step, holding on tightly.

A broad smile spread across Christopher Rabbit's face.

"I thought you weren't going to come," he shouted.

"It wasn't my fault," Hector replied, coming to an abrupt stop. Caravan Bear and Whitby were

thrown off the step. "I told them we'd be late picking you up but they kept adding more and more stuff."

"Hello, Christopher Rabbit," Whitby barked, running around him.

"Hello, Christopher Rabbit. Have you got your bags packed?" asked Caravan Bear.

Hector groaned.

"It's only one bag. A small bag," Christopher Rabbit explained. "I'll just go and get it."

He ran inside his house and returned almost at once with his bag.

"Right then," said Hector briskly as Christopher Rabbit climbed the steps. "Let's go!"

"Here, there, wherever the fancy takes us!" shouted Whitby as the caravan set off.

They had just left the village when Christopher Rabbit put his paw to his head. "Oh dear! I'm afraid I've left my Bible behind. When you didn't come, I put it back on the bookshelf."

Caravan Bear pulled on the reins and Hector came to a stop.

"What now?" the horse asked grumpily.

"Christopher Rabbit's left his Bible at home," Caravan Bear explained.

"Well, he'll have to go without it," Hector said firmly.

"He can't do that!" Whitby was shocked. "It wouldn't be a holiday without Christopher Rabbit reading us stories from the Bible."

"It might be a holiday for *you*," said Hector. "But it isn't for *me*. I'm not going anywhere."

And he sat down in the middle of the road.

It took a lot of coaxing on the part of Caravan Bear to persuade Hector to return to Christopher

Rabbit's burrow to collect the Bible. Christopher Rabbit kept saying how sorry he was, while Whitby thought it all very funny.

"If anything else has been left behind, it will have to stay left behind," Hector said grimly as they left Christopher Rabbit's home for the second time.

No one was in much of a holiday mood.

As they had set off so late it was soon getting dark, so Caravan Bear decided to pull off the road and stop for the night.

They sat outside on the steps and ate their supper in silence.

"I left my favourite ball behind," Whitby complained suddenly. "We haven't come very far, so can we...?"

"No!" snapped Hector. "Absolutely not! If we go home, then we stay home."

Christopher Rabbit looked around at his friends. They were angry and miserable.

"Would you like me to read you a story?" he asked shyly.

Hector snorted. "Might as well, as we had to go back for your Bible."

Christopher Rabbit went inside to fetch his book. "I'll tell you the story about what happened to Moses and the Israelites, who were God's chosen people, in the desert," he said when he returned.

He opened the book.

"If you remember, Moses finally persuaded the king of Egypt to free the Israelites. He had kept them as slaves."*

"Wasn't that only after God had sent some horrible plagues on the Egyptians?" Caravan Bear remembered.

"Yes – didn't the king keep saying he'd let the slaves go and then keep changing his mind?" Whitby added in a louder voice.

"And even after he let them go, he sent his army after them on horseback to bring them back," Hector reminded them, speaking even more loudly.

"And God made a path through the sea so that the Israelites could walk through on dry land," Caravan Bear added.

"But when the Egyptians tried to follow, their army drowned!" Whitby shouted triumphantly.

"Can't you keep your voices down?" hooted an owl from a nest in a nearby tree. "My little ones are trying to sleep!"

"I thought owls were awake at night," muttered Whitby.

"So what happened next?" Hector asked.

"Well, there they were," Christopher Rabbit said in a quiet voice, "hundreds, maybe thousands of Israelites, carrying just what they had managed to get hold of before they left Egypt…"

"Not like us, taking everything plus the kitchen sink…" muttered Hector.

"We didn't bring the kitchen sink," Caravan Bear corrected him.

"Only because it was plumbed in," Whitby added.

"You know what I mean."

"There they were, in the desert," Christopher Rabbit went on. "Not knowing where they were going…"

"Bit like us," said Hector.

"We do know where we're going," said Caravan Bear. "We're on holiday."

"It's fun for us, but it wasn't for the Israelites," Christopher Rabbit remarked. "They weren't on holiday and didn't have a home to go back to. All they knew was that Moses had told them God would lead them to a land called Canaan, a country God had promised to give them."

"Weren't they frightened?" asked Whitby.

"I'm sure they were. God told Moses that he wouldn't take the Israelites by the most direct way to Canaan. He would take them by a longer route through the desert. God led the way in what looked to the people like a pillar of cloud in the daytime and a pillar of fire at night. Whenever the cloud or the fire moved, the Israelites followed, and when it stopped, they also stopped and put up their tents."

"I suppose they didn't have satnavs in those days," Hector remarked.

"I'd rather rely on God than a satnav," said Whitby.

"We haven't got a satnav anyway," Caravan Bear reminded him.

"After the king's army drowned, did he try anything else to get his slaves back?" Whitby asked.

"No," said Christopher Rabbit. "The Israelites were free but had a long journey in front of them with no idea when it would end. It must have been hard walking in the desert with the sun beating down, and soon they began to grumble. They complained to Moses. 'Why did you bring us here? We're hungry and we're thirsty and we were better off as slaves in Egypt!'"

"That was a bit ungrateful after all Moses had done for them," Hector remarked.

"After all *God* had done for them," Caravan Bear corrected. "It was God who had made sure they were set free and God who was leading the way in the desert."

"What did they do for food?" asked Whitby.

"Moses told them that God would provide. That night, huge flocks of quails flew over their tents."

"What are quails?"

"I think they're birds," said Hector.

"Well, they wouldn't be fish flying over the tents, would they?" Whitby said sarcastically.

"So what was the point of the quails?" Hector asked.

"The quails landed by the tents and the Israelites caught and ate them," Christopher Rabbit replied. "So they had a good meal in the evening. And in the morning, the ground was covered with dew. When it dried, it was white and flaky. The Israelites tasted it. It tasted like sweet thin honey cakes. They called it 'manna'."

"Did we bring any manna with us?" asked Whitby. "It sounds delicious."

"No." said Caravan Bear, "We don't have any cakes either, but we did bring some ordinary biscuits."

He went into the caravan and returned with a plateful.

"Nice," said Whitby, her mouth full. "But I bet manna tasted better because it came from God."

"Everything comes from God," said Caravan Bear firmly.

"God told the Israelites to take just enough food for one day and eat it all up," said Christopher Rabbit.

"So there's no need to be greedy, Whitby, and eat up all those biscuits now," said Caravan Bear, frowning. "Leave some for another time."

"Oh, all right," said Whitby, her paw hovering over the one remaining biscuit. She left it on the plate and Hector promptly took it. Whitby pulled a face.

"I wasn't greedy, I was hungry," Hector explained. He crunched up the last bit of biscuit. Delicious. "Go on with the story, Christopher Rabbit."

"Can I have a drink first?" asked Whitby.

Caravan Bear fetched drinks for everyone.

"What did the Israelites drink?" asked Whitby. "I bet they were thirsty walking in the desert."

"In one place they stopped by a pool, but when they tried drinking the water, it tasted horrible. God told Moses to throw a piece of wood into the water and the nasty taste vanished – and they all drank.

"When they walked on to the next camp, there wasn't any water at all and everyone was angry with Moses. 'Give us water,' they shouted. 'Why did you bring us here to die of thirst?' Even by this time, they still didn't believe God was with them at all. Moses was frightened as some of them picked up stones, ready to throw them at him."

"I'd have been frightened too," Hector said.

"What did Moses do?" Caravan Bear asked.

"I expect he asked God for advice," said Christopher Rabbit. He looked down at his Bible. "Yes, that's what he did. He said, 'What can I do with these people?' God told Moses to take his staff – the one he used to part the waters of the Red Sea – and go with the leaders of the people to a rock that God would show him. He should strike the rock with his staff. Moses did that and clean fresh water spurted out. More than enough for everyone to drink."

He closed the Bible. "And that's the end of that part of the story."

Everyone was quiet for a while.

"How long were they wandering in the desert?" Caravan Bear asked.

Christopher Rabbit opened his Bible again. "Forty years."

"Forty years?" squeaked Whitby. "Wow! And all that time they just ate that manna and the odd quail? I bet they got pretty bored with it."

"Oh, I don't know," said Hector. "I just eat grass and oats and the odd carrot or apple if Caravan Bear gives me one."

"I expect they did get bored with it," Christopher Rabbit agreed. "But it was better than starving to death."

"I'm sure God could have provided some other food for them to eat," Whitby thought. "I mean, forty years is a long time."

"I'm sure he could, but God isn't a chef."

"Well, I'm just glad we brought lots of food with us," said Whitby smugly.

"Fancy wandering in the desert for forty years with a lot of complaining Israelites," Caravan Bear said thoughtfully. "Never getting any thanks. Just grumbles. Poor Moses."

"I've been away for less than a day with a lot of grumbling animals," said Hector, "so I don't know how Moses put up with it."

"We weren't the only ones grumbling," said Whitby. "You grumbled most."

"Perhaps we should stop grumbling and just be grateful that we've come away on holiday with plenty of everything," Caravan Bear said firmly.

Everyone was tired.

"Shall we start again and try not to grumble?" yawned Whitby sleepily.

"Let's," said Caravan Bear.

"I wonder why the Israelites didn't trust God to look after them," muttered Hector as he wandered off.

"I don't think any of us trust God enough," Christopher Rabbit said.

Whitby and Caravan Bear went inside but Christopher Rabbit lingered on the caravan steps for a moment, watching Hector on the far side of the field, his coat dappled by silver moonlight.

"Thank you for the story, God, and help us to trust you more. Thank you for everything you provide for us and especially for my friends."

He stayed where he was for a moment more, and then went into the caravan and closed the door.

God's Ten Laws

It was a steep hill. A very steep hill.

It was hot. Very hot.

Hector slowly towed the caravan up the dusty road. As he went, he grumbled under his breath.

"Shouldn't be towing a caravan in this heat, especially a heavy caravan. This is the third hill I've been up today. It might be a holiday for Caravan Bear, Whitby, and Christopher Rabbit, but it's not much of a holiday for me."

Sitting on the top step of the caravan, holding the reins, Caravan Bear overheard Hector's grumbles.

"I'm sorry about this, Hector, but just wait until we get to the top. There'll be a wonderful view."

"There'd better be."

Whitby jumped off the step.

"Come on, Hector, you can do it!" she called encouragingly. "Race you to the top!"

"That's not fair – you're not towing a caravan!"

Whitby laughed and ran on ahead.

"All right," Hector said, gritting his teeth. "I'll show you!"

With that, he set off at a run, the caravan bouncing behind him.

A few minutes later, he reached the top. He stopped with a jerk, sending everything in the caravan, including Caravan Bear and Christopher Rabbit, flying.

"Not bad for an old horse," Hector said happily, and he began grazing on the lush green grass around him. Meanwhile, Caravan Bear, Christopher Rabbit, and Whitby put everything back in its place inside the caravan and secured the wheels to make sure it didn't roll back down the hill.

When they had finished, they looked around.

Christopher Rabbit shaded his eyes with his paw. "What a wonderful view!"

Far below them, the countryside was spread out

like a map. Green fields, small villages, winding ribbons of roads, rolling hills, and woodland. Far in the distance they could see the sea sparkling blue under the bright spring sunshine.

Whitby ran around barking excitedly. "I like it here. Can we go and explore?"

And that's what they did – apart from Hector, who felt he had done enough walking for one day.

"I'll come and explore tomorrow!" he shouted as Christopher Rabbit, Caravan Bear, and Whitby disappeared over the brow of the hill.

But when they woke up the next morning, none of them felt like exploring. The hill was covered in thick grey-white clouds. When they went outside, it felt wet and cold.

"What shall we do?" asked Caravan Bear glumly as they returned to the caravan and sat looking out at the sea of white.

"Could we move somewhere else?" Christopher Rabbit suggested.

"Yes, let's," Whitby agreed.

"I'm not moving another step," Hector said firmly. "You said I could have a rest when we reached the top of the hill, and a rest I'm having."

"In any case, it would be a bit dangerous," said Caravan Bear thoughtfully, "as Hector wouldn't be able to see where he was going."

"Just what I was going to say," Hector agreed.

"Shall we play a game?" Caravan Bear suggested.

No one said anything.

"Would you like me to tell you a story from the Bible?" Christopher Rabbit asked, looking around at their glum faces. "What's happened to us makes me think of when Moses went up a mountain to talk to God."

Hector nodded. "That's a good idea."

The others agreed.

"You remember Moses leading God's chosen people out of slavery in Egypt?" Christopher Rabbit began.

"They spent years in the desert and all they did was grumble," said Whitby.

"That's right. Well, they finally arrived at the foot of a big mountain."

"Like this one?" Whitby asked.

"This isn't a mountain, it's a hill," Caravan Bear corrected.

"Felt like a mountain to me," muttered Hector.

"The name of the mountain was Mount Sinai," Christopher Rabbit went on. "They set up camp and waited while Moses climbed to the top to ask God what they should do next."

"Did God live at the top of the mountain?" Caravan Bear asked.

"I don't think God lives anywhere especially," Christopher Rabbit thought aloud. "But perhaps Moses felt that he would be nearer to God on the mountaintop than down at the camp."

"I expect it was quieter up there," Hector agreed.

"Away from all those grumbling Israelites," Whitby added.

"Anyway, when Moses reached the top, God told him to tell the Israelites that he wanted to make an agreement with them. It was called a covenant. He would carry on being their God and looking after them if they would agree to follow his ways."

Caravan Bear nodded his head. "Seems reasonable."

"Moses went down the mountain and told the people what God had said. They said they would like to make this covenant with God, so Moses went back up the mountain again."

"I bet he was tired going up and down the mountain," Whitby said sympathetically.

"At least he wasn't towing a caravan," snorted Hector.

"Where does God live?" Caravan Bear asked.

"I think God is everywhere," Christopher Rabbit replied.

"If that's the case, why did Moses have to go tramping up and down the mountain to tell God what had happened?"

Christopher Rabbit shook his head. "I don't know."

"Do you think that when this story was written, people thought that God lived at the top of a mountain?" Hector asked.

"Could be."

"Or might it be that mountains were thought to be holy places where God could meet with people?" asked Caravan Bear.

"Perhaps because it was a hard climb to get to the top," Hector wondered.

"Was it steep?" asked Whitby.

Christopher Rabbit looked up. "What?"

"The mountain."

"Oh, I expect so."

"If it was anything like the hills I've been up, it was very steep," Hector commented.

"So perhaps we might meet God *here*," Whitby suggested, looking out of the window at the mist swirling outside the caravan.

"We don't have to climb up a hill or a mountain to meet God," said Christopher Rabbit firmly. He went on with the story. "God gave Moses ten commandments, or laws, for the Israelites to follow.

"The first four laws told the people how they should treat God. They were to praise and serve only the one true God. The Israelites were not to make idols and try to worship them. God's name was to be treated with respect. And the fourth commandment told them to rest on the seventh day of the week."

"I like that last one," Hector said positively.

"What did God mean about idols?" asked Whitby.

"Statues and things…?" Caravan Bear wondered.

"Perhaps God meant more than statues," Christopher Rabbit said thoughtfully. "Perhaps idols are everything we value too much and think more important than God. Things like…"

"Money? A lot of people seem to want lots of money," Hector suggested. "I know my old master did."

"I know what Caravan Bear worships," said Whitby, grinning. "It's the caravan."

"No, it's not!," Caravan Bear retorted sharply. "It's not that it's more important than God. It's just – well… I don't worship it but I do like it and I like to look after it."

"I know what Whitby worships," Hector said with a loud snort. "Food and her toys."

"Well, what about you?" Whitby replied angrily. "You worship a… a…" She fell silent as she couldn't think of anything. "… a bag of oats," she said at last.

"I think we all worship things and put our trust in them rather than in God," Christopher Rabbit said slowly. "I know I don't trust God enough."

"You said there were ten commandments," said Hector. "We've had four, so what were the other six?"

"They were how we should treat each other," Christopher Rabbit replied. "The first one was not to hurt or look down on your parents but to show them respect."

"I don't know who my parents were," Hector said. "I think I was sold when I was very little."

"That's sad," said Whitby. "I'll try to be very nice to you to make up for it."

"Thank you." They smiled at each other.

"The other laws were not to murder; not to run off with anyone else's husband or wife; not to steal; not to tell lies; and not to be jealous of the things that belong to others."

"Well, there's a law I've often broken," said Whitby.

"Which one?" Christopher Rabbit asked.

"Not being jealous. Do you remember all those lovely toys we saw when we met Ermintrude the poodle? A whole room filled with them! I felt very jealous."*

"They are all very sensible laws, but they're not always easy to keep, are they?" Caravan Bear said thoughtfully.

"Why do we need commandments anyway?" Hector asked.

"Think what a mess we'd all be in if we didn't have any," Caravan Bear replied.

"I think if we didn't have any laws from God, we'd all go around doing just what we wanted without thinking about anyone else," Christopher Rabbit said.

"What happened next?" asked Hector.

"A storm broke over the mountain. The mountain was covered in fire and smoke and began to shake. Everyone was terrified. Moses came down from the mountain and told the people what God had said. Everyone agreed to obey God's laws. God said he'd write them on large flat stones for the people to keep, so Moses went back up the mountain to collect them. He was gone a long time as God gave him many other laws."

"What sort of laws?"

"Oh, about right and wrong, about health, about punishment, about the kind of feasts and worship

God wanted his people to share. He carved the ten most important laws himself into two stone tablets and Moses picked them up and started back down the mountain once more."

"He must have been very fit with all the exercise he was getting," Whitby said.

"I expect he was," agreed Christopher Rabbit. "Unfortunately he'd been gone for a long time and everyone waiting in the camp had become bored and angry. 'Why has he been away for so long?' they asked. 'Perhaps he's not going to come back. Let's have a new god and follow him instead.'

"They melted down all the gold they had and made an enormous golden calf. They bowed down in front of it, and then held a feast to celebrate."

"Whoever heard of anyone bowing down before a statue!" Hector scoffed.

"I think quite a lot of people do," Christopher Rabbit said.

"People are stupid, aren't they?" Whitby wrinkled her nose. "You wouldn't get animals bowing to statues."

"Isn't that the same as the worship of them?" Caravan Bear wondered.

"And we've all said that we worship things more than God. It doesn't have to be golden statues," Christopher Rabbit said thoughtfully. "So I don't think we should say that the Israelites were stupid."

"What happened when Moses got back down the mountain?" Caravan Bear asked.

"He was furious. He threw down the tablets and they broke into little pieces. Then he ground up the golden idol until it was dust. 'You've done a dreadful thing!' he told the people. That frightened them."

"Wasn't God angry as well?" Caravan Bear asked.

"Of course he was. So Moses went back up the mountain and asked God to forgive the people and give them a second chance. And because God loved them, as he loves us, he forgave them and wrote out the laws for a second time on two new stone tablets.

"When Moses returned to the camp, the people said they were sorry. They listened quietly as he taught them the laws of God, and the covenant agreement between God and his people was sealed."

Christopher Rabbit closed the Bible and everyone was silent for a while.

Caravan Bear glanced out of the window. "The cloud's lifting!"

They ran to the door. A fresh wind was blowing and the clouds were drifting away. A patch of blue appeared and suddenly the sun burst out.

"Thank you, God, for the covenant you made with your people," Christopher Rabbit said. "Help us to try and keep your laws."

"I'm glad to know that you don't live on top of a mountain," Whitby added.

"So am I," Hector agreed wholeheartedly.

In the Lions' Den

"Oh look!" Whitby exclaimed as she, Caravan Bear, and Christopher Rabbit sat on the top step of the caravan as Hector clip-clopped along the road. "Look at that notice!"

"What notice?" asked Caravan Bear, jerking awake out of a gentle doze. It was a hot day and the caravan swayed from side to side as, for once, Hector was moving quite slowly.

"It says there's a safari park just past the next village. Can we go to it?"

"What's a safari park?" asked Christopher Rabbit.

"It's a place where they keep lots of different animals and people drive around and look at them," said Caravan Bear.

"Why?" Whitby asked.

"Because they want to see them, I suppose."

"Do you think they've got lions and tigers?" Whitby asked Caravan Bear excitedly.

"Probably."

"I'd like to see a lion."

"It would eat you in one mouthful," said Hector. He slowed to a stop. "How much further are we going?"

Caravan Bear looked at his map. "I think there's a wood just around the bend in the road. We'll stop there. It'll be nice and cool."

The friends stopped in a sunlit glade and set up their caravan. When they had been for a walk and eaten some supper, Whitby asked again.

"Can we go to the safari park tomorrow?"

"The owners might want to keep you and put you on show in a cage," Hector grinned.

"Do you think so?"

"He's only teasing," said Caravan Bear.

"I'm only teasing," Hector agreed. "Who would want to show off a dog like you?"

"And they don't put animals in cages in a safari park. They're free to wander around," Caravan Bear explained.

Whitby looked around. "I hope there aren't any lions wandering around here."

"I thought you wanted to see one," Hector said.

"Read us a story, Christopher Rabbit, or they'll be arguing all evening," sighed Caravan Bear.

Christopher Rabbit, Whitby, and Caravan Bear went inside while Hector poked his nose in through the window. Christopher Rabbit picked up his Bible.

"How about a story with lions in it?" he asked.

"As long as it's not frightening," Whitby replied.

Christopher Rabbit opened the book. "The king of Persia, Darius the Great, ruled over a large empire. Because it was so large, he divided it into a hundred and twenty provinces. Each province was ruled by a governor and he chose three supervisors to be in charge of the governors."

"Where do the lions come in?" asked Hector.

"Later in the story."

"Can't you get to it a bit more quickly? I get confused with lots of numbers."

"You need to know the background," Christopher Rabbit explained, a bit hurt. "One of these three supervisors was Daniel, who was a Jewish believer, a friend of God. He was one of the many people

41

who had been taken to live in Babylonia when the land of the Israelites had been taken over by the Babylonian army.

"Daniel was good at his job. He was hardworking and loyal to the king. He was such a good supervisor that the king soon planned to put him in charge over everyone. That made the other two supervisors and the hundred and twenty governors jealous."

"Why?" asked Whitby.

"Probably because they all wanted to be in charge."

"They couldn't *all* be in charge of everyone and everything," Whitby said. Hector agreed.

"Caravan Bear is in charge of the caravan, I'm in charge of towing it, Christopher Rabbit is in charge of entertaining us with his stories, and Whitby…"

"Isn't in charge of anything," Whitby finished happily.

"They probably didn't think of that," Christopher Rabbit said thoughtfully. "They might also have been jealous of Daniel because he was different. Although he'd lived in Babylonia for years, he still worshipped the one true God of the Jews."

"Didn't the others worship God?" Caravan Bear asked.

"They followed a different religion," Christopher Rabbit replied. "So they got together and began to make a plan. They wanted to turn the king against Daniel and get rid of him. They watched him carefully, but Daniel was honest and trustworthy – and the king thought very highly of him. The plotters had to think of something else and soon came up with another, quite clever plot. Knowing Daniel was very religious and prayed three times a day to God, they went to speak to the king.

"'O great King Darius, may you live for ever!' one of them said."

"Trying to flatter him," Caravan Bear said, disapprovingly.

"'We feel that you should issue a decree. Anyone found praying to anyone, divine or human, other than you, O King, should be thrown into a den of lions. This decree should last for thirty days.'"

"Did the king agree?" asked Whitby.

"Yes, he did."

"Why?"

"I expect he was flattered," said Hector.

Whitby turned toward him. "What do you mean?"

"Well, some humans like to be thought as important as God, don't they?"

"*More* important sometimes," agreed Christopher Rabbit. "Remember the story of the Tower of Babel."*

"So what happened next?"

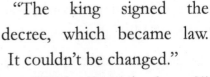

"The king signed the decree, which became law. It couldn't be changed."

"Did Daniel know?" asked Whitby.

"Oh yes. He knew about it, but to him God was more important than King Darius. So three times a day, just as before, he went to his house – which had windows that looked toward Jerusalem – and he got down on his knees and prayed to God.

"The plotters watched him, and then, very pleased with themselves, went to the king.

44

" 'O King,' they said, 'Didn't you sign a decree saying that within the next thirty days anyone who prays to anyone divine or human apart from you should be thrown into a den of lions?'

" 'Yes,' said the king.

" 'Well,' they said triumphantly, 'Daniel has been saying his prayers three times a day – not to you, but to his God.'

"The king was very upset when he heard this and spent all day trying to work out a way to save Daniel. But the plotters knew that the law the king had made was a law of the Medes and Persians. It was binding and couldn't be changed."

"Who were the Medes?" asked Caravan Bear.

"I think they were a people who lived in a country called Media. They once had a large empire but were conquered by Persia," Christopher Rabbit replied.

"Bit stupid, wasn't he?" said Hector.

"Who?" replied Christopher Rabbit, who was still thinking about the Medes.

"King Darius, of course. You'd have thought he would have known he'd been tricked into condemning his friend to death."

"You'd have thought so. But he didn't," Christopher Rabbit replied. "The plotters brought the order for Daniel's death to the king, and the king had to sign it."

"Why?" asked Whitby.

"Why what?"

"Why did he have to sign it? As he was king, he could have changed the law, couldn't he? Torn it up. I mean, he was in charge."

The animals thought about this.

"I don't think you can do that," Christopher Rabbit said slowly.

"Why not?"

"Even kings have to keep to the law," said Caravan Bear.

"Think of the ten laws God gave Moses," agreed Christopher Rabbit. "Though I agree the king was a bit stupid. He was very unhappy about it and went with Daniel down to the den where the lions lived."

"I bet that made Daniel feel a whole lot better," Hector said sarcastically.

"Was the king more upset than Daniel?" wondered Caravan Bear.

"Shouldn't think so," said Whitby. "I mean, the

king could look forward to going back to his palace for a tasty meal. All poor old Daniel could look forward to was *being* a tasty meal for a bunch of hungry lions."

"I expect Daniel was scared, but he probably felt that he was doing what God wanted. Perhaps that gave him strength," Caravan Bear suggested.

"Perhaps," said Christopher Rabbit. "Anyway, the king told Daniel, 'May your God, whom you so faithfully serve, rescue you now!'"

"Oh, that's so sad!" Whitby said, her eyes filling with tears.

"Daniel went into the den…"

"I expect he could hear the lions roaring," said Hector.

"I expect he could. A large stone was rolled against the mouth and it was sealed by the king's own signet ring. Then the king went home to his palace. He was so upset that he couldn't eat and he couldn't sleep."

"I have no sympathy for him," said Hector decisively. "I hope he had a terrible night!"

"This is a good story," said Whitby.

"As soon as it grew light, the king got up…"

"I thought he hadn't been to bed?" Hector protested.

"It doesn't say in the Bible that he didn't go to bed, it just says that he couldn't sleep," Christopher Rabbit explained. "He got up and hurried to the lions' den…"

"Probably wanted to see whether the lions had eaten all of Daniel," Whitby said breathlessly, "or only bits."

"Depends how hungry they were," said Hector.

"I bet the plotters made sure the lions were hungry before Daniel was put into the den," Whitby answered.

"It's the sort of thing they'd have thought of," Hector agreed. "Go on, Christopher Rabbit."

"When he got near, he called out: 'Daniel, servant of the living God. Has your God been able to save you?'

"And he heard Daniel's voice from deep inside the den: 'O great king, my God sent his angel to close the lions' mouths so that they wouldn't hurt me. He did so because I have done nothing wrong.'

"Well, the king was overjoyed. He ordered his servants to move the stone and let Daniel out of the den. When he came out, he was completely unhurt."

"What about the plotters?" Whitby asked.

"I was coming to that. The king decided that all those who had accused Daniel should be thrown into the den and eaten by the lions."

"Good!" said Whitby. "Served them right!"

"And King Darius went further. He issued a proclamation in all the languages of his huge empire that Daniel's God, the God of the Jews, was the one, true, living God: the true God because he had saved the king's friend Daniel from the lions."

As Christopher Rabbit closed his Bible, there was the sound of scuffling outside the door.

"Are we expecting visitors?" Caravan Bear asked as he went to open it.

They heard a low roar.

"Don't open it!" Whitby said urgently.

"Don't be ridiculous!"

Caravan Bear opened the door and gasped. A large lion with a splendid mane of golden fur filled the doorway.

"I s... s... said you shouldn't open the door!" squeaked Whitby, taking a flying leap on to the top of the cupboard.

The lion looked around.

"I'm sorry to bother you," he said politely,

"but have you seen my youngest cub, Florrie? She wandered off some hours ago and my wife and I are very worried about her."

"N... no..." Caravan Bear stammered. "We... we've been in here all evening listening to Christopher Rabbit read a story from his Bible."

"It was about a lion," Christopher Rabbit said nervously. "Quite a few lions, in fact, who didn't eat Daniel."

"Oh, really? That sounds very interesting," said the lion. "I'd like to hear it sometime, but at the moment I really must find Florrie. If you see her, could you let me know? We're not very far away – just at the safari park down the road."

"How did you get out?" asked Caravan Bear curiously. He'd stopped being afraid of such a polite lion.

"Not easy but not impossible," replied the lion vaguely.

"Don't you want to eat us?" Whitby asked bravely.

"Not just now," the lion said gently. "I've had my dinner. They look after us very well at the park." He looked up at Whitby, who was still squashed between the cupboard and the ceiling. "And, if you don't mind my saying so, you wouldn't make much of a meal."

There was a sound outside the caravan. It was Hector, who had galloped off as soon as he had seen the lion.

"Is this who you're looking for?" Hector asked breathlessly, coming to a stop beside the caravan's steps. Perched on his back was a very small lion cub.

"Oh, Florrie, you naughty girl!" said the lion. He turned to Hector, Caravan Bear, Christopher Rabbit, and Whitby.

"Thank you so much," he said. "All of you. Perhaps you'd like to visit the safari park tomorrow? I'll introduce you to the other animals, and if you bring your Bible, you could tell us a story."

With that, he picked his cub up gently between his teeth and walked off.

"Phew!" exclaimed Whitby, coming down from the cupboard. "We won't go, will we, Caravan Bear?"

"Why not?"

"I thought you *wanted* to go," Hector teased.

"Thank you, God, for sending us a friendly lion who didn't want to eat us," said Christopher Rabbit as he watched the lion walk off through the wood.

"And thank you for the story of Daniel," Caravan Bear added.

David and the Giant

Hector pulled the caravan up to the gates of the safari park.

A man in uniform came to meet them. "Sorry, you're too late. We're just closing."

"We've not come to visit the park, we've come to see a friend," said Caravan Bear, letting go of the reins.

"We've been invited," Whitby added, prancing around the man's legs.

"Oh yes?" said the man suspiciously. "Who invited you, then?"

"The lion," Caravan Bear answered.

The man scratched his head. "Well, it's very irregular, very irregular indeed – but I suppose if the

54

lion invited you… You'll have to stay the night, as once we've locked up, you won't be able to get out."

"That's all right," Caravan Bear assured him. "That's why we've brought the caravan."

The man waved them through.

As they drove through the park, the friends looked around with interest. They saw all kinds of animals, many they'd never seen before. A couple of tall and stately-looking giraffes walked past, nodding their long necks when they saw the caravan.

"Evening," said one.

"Don't you know the park is closed to visitors?" said the other.

"We're looking for the lion," Caravan Bear explained.

"Oh, you mean Wilfred," said the first giraffe. She looked around. "Anyone seen Wilfred?"

A tiger padded out from a clump of trees.

"He's over by the lake. He said we were all to meet there." The tiger looked at Whitby and opened his mouth to show a set of very sharp teeth. Whitby ran behind Christopher Rabbit.

"Do… do you think we should have come?" she asked in a small voice.

"Bit late to turn back now," said Hector. "The gates have been locked."

He turned toward the lake and plodded on, the caravan bouncing on the rough grass behind him.

Wilfred came to meet them, a beaming smile on his face. "Thank you for coming – we're all so grateful." Behind him were three large elephants.

From the mud beside the lake rose a water buffalo. He shook himself, shedding mud and water onto a group of penguins who were waddling in their direction. Above them, a group of monkeys were swinging down from the trees, chattering noisily as they landed on the caravan roof. One of them landed on Hector.

Insects, reptiles, birds, and other animals were streaming in from all sides. There were zebras, more tigers, cattle with long horns, four black bears, a white rhinoceros, a jackal, and many more. Along the ground slithered a large snake with diamond markings on its back. A giant snail and an old tortoise slowly brought up the rear. Brightly coloured birds flew overhead around the caravan, tweeting and cawing. The noise was tremendous.

"I don't think I like this," said Whitby. Caravan Bear, Hector, and Christopher Rabbit agreed, but didn't say anything.

"If you'd like to park your caravan just here, we'll soon get everyone settled and you can tell your story," Wilfred said happily. "We're all looking forward to it."

The caravan was soon secured, but it took much longer for all the animals in the safari park to get settled. Arguments broke out about who should sit the closest.

"We elephants should, because we are the biggest beasts in the safari park," said one of the elephants. They tramped to the front.

"Here, watch out! You nearly stepped on me!" hissed the snake.

"Biggest isn't always best," squeaked Florrie the lion cub, as the elephant blocked her view.

"If you don't mind," Wilfred said politely to the elephant. He picked up the cub and placed her on Hector's back. The monkey, who was already sitting on Hector and pulling at his coat, laughed and swung onto the steps.

Wilfred turned to the animals.

"Now everyone, please settle down. Christopher Rabbit has very kindly offered to read us a story."

"Have I?" Christopher Rabbit thought as he looked around the wide circle of animals. They looked back at him expectantly. Some of them were very large, with massive jaws and teeth. Christopher Rabbit shuddered. He closed his eyes and wished with all his heart that he was back in his safe, cosy home. He even wished he had never come away on this adventure with Caravan Bear, Whitby, and Hector. What story would they all like? If they didn't like it, they might eat him. They might eat all of them! He was very, very frightened.

"Please help me, God," he thought.

He opened his eyes and suddenly knew which story to tell. He fetched his Bible, settled down on the top step of the caravan, and opened it.

"This is a story from a book called the Bible. It's got many wonderful stories in it."

The animals quietened down.

Christopher Rabbit took a deep breath and began: "The Israelites, the people of God, lived in the land of Canaan. Other people lived there, too, and sometimes it was difficult for them all to live together in peace. War had been declared between people called the Philistines and the Israelites. The Philistine army was camped on one hill. The Israelites were camped on another hill. There was a deep valley in between.

"A man called Jesse had three sons in the Israelite army. His youngest son, David, was too young to be fighting, so he had stayed at home to look after the sheep. Jesse, not hearing from his sons and worried about what was happening to them, called David and told him to go to find his brothers, take them food, and find out how the battle was going.

"David set off. When he arrived on the hill where the Israelites were camped, he heard a voice shouting loudly across the valley. David turned and saw the biggest man he'd ever seen. The man, whose name was Goliath, must have been about three metres high and was fully armed for battle. He was striding with giant steps up and down, up and down.

"'Come on, you Israelites!' he shouted. 'Choose a man to fight me! If he wins we'll become your slaves, but if I win then *you* will become *our* slaves!'"

"Would you mind speaking up a bit?" the snake interrupted. "I'm a bit hard of hearing."

Christopher Rabbit went on in a louder voice. "The Israelites were scared. None of them were big enough or brave enough to fight this enormous man. David watched for a bit and then found his brothers, gave them the food, and went home.

"Every day for forty days, morning and evening, Goliath walked backward and forward, issuing his challenge to the Israelites, shouting and making fun of them. No one would volunteer to fight him."

"Wish I'd been there," said the rhinoceros. "I'd have soon crushed that giant."

"I'd have torn him into little pieces," said the tiger, baring his teeth.

"Made mincemeat out of him," grinned the jackal.

Christopher Rabbit gulped. Some of the animals were very frightening indeed.

He went on. "A few days later, Jesse told David to go back to the camp with more food for his brothers. David left his sheep in the care of another shepherd, collected the food, and set off for the camp. He arrived just as the army were going into their battle positions.

"David ran to see his brothers. As he reached them, Goliath came out once more and shouted out his challenge in a loud voice. David listened for a while and then told his brothers that no one had the right to challenge the Israelites, who were God's people.

His brothers told him to go home. But someone had overheard David and told the king, whose name was Saul, what David had said. David was summoned to the king."

" 'Your Majesty,' David said. 'I'll fight the giant.'

" 'You?' King Saul replied. 'You're only a lad. What makes you think you can win?'

" 'God is on our side,' David said. He told the king that although he was young he had had good practice as a shepherd, killing lions and bears when they attacked his sheep. He was an excellent shot with a sling and a stone."

"I've gone off this David," said a large black bear.

"Just as well we've been fed and aren't hungry," said the tiger with a nasty smile.

The animals murmured their agreement.

"Who cares about a load of silly sheep anyway," said the jackal.

"Well, it was David's job to look after them and make sure they didn't come to any harm," Christopher Rabbit said nervously.

"We don't kill just for the sake of it," a leopard explained. "Not like humans with their wars."

Christopher Rabbit thought he'd better get on with the story. "King Saul agreed that David should fight Goliath. He dressed him in his own heavy armour and put his own helmet on David's head. David fastened the king's sword around his waist – but then he found that he couldn't walk as he was so weighed down. So he took off the king's clothes and sword and, dressed just in his tunic, picked up his shepherd's staff. He chose five smooth stones from a stream, put them in his bag, picked up a home-made sling, and slowly walked over to the giant.

"When Goliath saw David approach, he burst out laughing. Then he grew angry. 'How dare you think about fighting me! What's that stick for? Come here so that I can kill you and feed your flesh to the birds and wild animals!'"

Christopher Rabbit turned the page.

"What happened?" asked the water buffalo.

"David shouted back. 'You come against me with your sword and spear, but I come in the name of God, the God of Israel. He'll give me victory over you!'

"As Goliath moved forward to attack him, David took out a stone, fitted it into the sling, swung it around his head, and let it fly. It hit Goliath right in the middle of his forehead and the giant fell down, stunned. David ran over to him, picked up the giant's sword, and killed him. The Philistines turned and ran away. And that's the end of the story."

He closed the book.

"Just goes to show that biggest isn't always best," muttered the snake.

"Do you think David was frightened when he saw the giant come toward him?" asked the tortoise.

"Probably," said Christopher Rabbit. "But he knew that God was on his side and that made all the difference."

Everyone nodded. The animals began to move away, the water buffalo went back to his mud bath and the penguins slipped into the water. Some of the animals disappeared into the trees, the birds flying high above them, searching for nests for the night, while the giant snail glided away beside the tortoise.

"That was a good story," said Wilfred. "Thank you for telling it to us."

He picked Florrie up gently and walked off.

Christopher Rabbit, Caravan Bear, Hector, and Whitby were left alone. It was getting dark.

"Phew!" said Whitby, letting out her breath. "That could have been nasty, especially when you mentioned the lions and bears."

"It could have been," agreed Christopher Rabbit. He found his paws were shaking. "Thank you for looking after us, God."

"Weren't you scared?" asked Whitby curiously.

"Of course I was. But I asked God to help me and he did."

"Just as David must have done."

"I expect so."

"Do you think we'll be safe here tonight?" asked Hector.

"Oh, I think so," said Christopher Rabbit. "Whatever happens, God will be with us."

"Well, I'm hungry," Whitby declared. "What's for supper?"

And they went inside the caravan and shut the door.

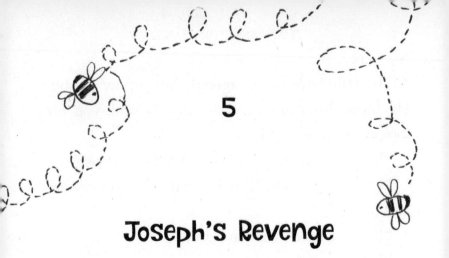

5

Joseph's Revenge

At first Caravan Bear thought he could hear a bee buzzing round and round as he sat on the top step of the caravan, reins in his hand, while Hector plodded along the dusty road.

"Can you hear that noise?" he asked Christopher Rabbit, who was sitting beside him. "Is it a bee?"

Christopher Rabbit listened. "I don't think it's a bee. It sounds as if there's something coming up behind us."

They both listened hard.

"It's not a car."

The sound grew louder.

And louder.

Then, with the blare of a horn and a whoosh of

dust, the caravan was overtaken. Hector, alarmed at the sudden noise, swerved toward a bank.

"What was that?" Whitby asked, running out of the caravan to join Caravan Bear and Christopher Rabbit.

"It was a motorbike," Hector called angrily, "being driven very dangerously. Ought to be banned from the road," he muttered as he set off again.

A mile or so later on they saw the motorbike leaning against a gate leading into a field. Sitting on top of the gate was a large pink pig wearing a crash helmet. He was waving at them vigorously.

Hector slowed. "It can't be…" he muttered.

"It is…" Caravan Bear cried.

"Not…" Whitby began.

"Hello, hello!" called the pig. "I guessed you'd come this way!"

"… Runt!" Whitby finished.

Runt took off his helmet.

"That's right! It's me! Turning up like a bad penny!"

"You said it," Whitby muttered.

Caravan Bear, Christopher Rabbit, Hector, and Whitby had met Runt before on their previous caravan adventures.*

"Hello, Runt," said Caravan Bear. "How are you?"

"As you see!" Runt beamed. "Gave you a surprise, didn't I?"

"Yes," Hector said sourly. "You did."

Christopher Rabbit scrambled down the caravan steps. "I've never seen a pig ride a motorbike before."

"I'm not surprised. I expect I'm the only motor-bike-riding pig in the world," Runt boasted.

"Is it your bike?" asked Whitby.

"No. It belongs to the farmer, but he said I could ride it whenever I want."

"He did?"

Runt puffed out his chest.

"'Runtie,' he said. That's the name he calls me. 'Runtie, what's mine is yours!'"

"Why did he say that?" asked Whitby.

"Because I made him rich. I made him the richest farmer in the area. 'Try pigs,' I said to him. 'Turn the farm into a pig farm and you can't go wrong!' He took my advice and there you are. Never looked back."

"I see," said Caravan Bear, feeling a bit overwhelmed. "Well, it's been very good meeting you again, Runt, but we must be getting on. We have some way to go tonight."

"No, you haven't. You're staying here, on this field."

He hopped down from the gate and pushed it wide open.

"It's all fixed up with the farmer."

"Well, that's very nice of you but…"

"But nothing. I want to hear the end of the story you started telling me but didn't finish."

"Oh. Which story?"

"The one about Joseph, of course. You know, the one with all those dreadful brothers who threw him into a pit, then dragged him out and sold him as a slave."

Christopher Rabbit, Caravan Bear, Whitby, and Hector looked at Runt in amazement.

"You have a good memory," Christopher Rabbit said.

Runt shrugged his enormous shoulders. "That's why I'm top hog here. The farmer can't do without me."

He looked at Christopher Rabbit. "You *have* brought your Bible with you, haven't you?"

"Oh yes."

"Well, let's hear it, then."

"After supper," said Caravan Bear firmly. "We've first got to get the caravan set up, fetch some water, and have something to eat."

"Supper!" Runt said. "That sounds a good idea. You set up and I'll be back for something to eat. I have a few important things to do first."

With that, he jumped on the motorbike and roared off up the field. Everyone watched him go.

"Well…" Hector began.

"He hasn't changed a bit," said Caravan Bear.

"Apart from getting fatter and more full of himself," said Whitby.

True to his word, Runt appeared just as the friends were settling down to their supper.

"Well, this is all very nice," Runt said, squashing himself down between Caravan Bear and Christopher Rabbit and grabbing a handful of biscuits. "I was only saying to my wife the other day that I was sure you'd come along."

"Your wife?" Whitby asked, spluttering over a biscuit.

"Oh yes. Married and with a litter of piglets. Not all of them as clever as I was at their age but one or two might be promising," he added.

"I'm sure they'll all turn out well," Caravan Bear said faintly.

Runt laughed. "Not as well as their father."

After every scrap of food had been eaten, mostly by Runt, Christopher Rabbit took down his Bible and found the right place while Runt looked around the caravan with pleasure.

"This is very nice," he said. "Very nice indeed. A meeting of old friends, a good supper, and now a story. What could be better?"

At these words, Christopher Rabbit and Caravan Bear looked at each other, a little ashamed of the nasty things they'd said about Runt in the past. Hector poked his head in through the window, chewing a mouthful of grass, while Whitby – curled up on her favourite cushion – was not the least bit ashamed of the nasty things she'd said about Runt.

"Get on with it, Christopher Rabbit," she urged.

"Joseph, as Runt remembered, was sold to some slave dealers who were on their way to Egypt. When the brothers returned home, they told their father, Jacob, that Joseph was dead. Once in Egypt, Joseph was bought by a captain of the king's guard called Potiphar. Joseph was good at his work and Potiphar soon put him in charge of his household.

"Unfortunately, Potiphar's wife accused him of things he didn't do, and he ended up in prison. He might have stayed there if he hadn't used the gift God had given him to help people understand what their dreams meant."

"God's given me lots of gifts," Runt broke in importantly. "And of course I'm very grateful to him. Mind you, I think I'd have been very gifted anyway even without God's help."

"How did Joseph get out of prison?" Hector asked.

"Pharaoh – that's the king of Egypt – had a dream. He dreamed that he was standing by the River Nile and saw seven fat and healthy cows come out of the river and start grazing among the reeds. They were followed by seven thin and hungry cows who came out of the river and ate the seven fat cows. Pharaoh woke up, then fell asleep again – and had another dream.

"This time he saw seven healthy heads of grain growing on a single stalk. After them sprouted seven other heads of grain that were thin and

scorched by the east wind. The thin heads of grain swallowed the healthy heads of grain."

"Let me see," Runt interrupted. "It's like a puzzle – and I'm very good at solving puzzles."

"Is there anything you're not good at?" Whitby asked.

Runt thought about it. "I don't think so. Now be quiet while I work out the answer."

He screwed up his face as he thought.

"Something to do with seven," he said at last.

"That's pretty obvious." said Whitby sarcastically. "Any other ideas?"

"Just give me a minute."

Everyone was silent.

"Well, I don't think it's very hard to explain," Hector said impatiently. "Pharaoh must have eaten too much the night before – that's why he had bad dreams."

"They weren't really bad dreams," said Caravan Bear. "They were just strange."

"No one in Pharaoh's court could interpret his dreams," Christopher Rabbit went on. "Then Pharaoh's cup-bearer remembered that while they had both been in prison, Joseph had explained a dream he had had. He told Pharaoh this and Joseph was sent for. After a wash and a change of clothes…"

"It couldn't have been very clean in the prison," Whitby remarked.

"And he would have had to look smart if he was going to meet Pharaoh," Runt said decisively. "I'm always telling my piglets that the way to get on in life is to look smart."

"'I'm told you can interpret dreams,' Pharaoh said to Joseph.

"'I can't,' Joseph replied. 'But God can.'

"When Pharaoh told Joseph what he had seen in his dreams, Joseph explained to him what they meant. 'It's quite simple, your Majesty,' he said. 'Both dreams are the same. God has revealed to you what's going to happen. The seven fat cows and seven healthy heads of grain will mean there will be seven years of plenty for Egypt. Good harvests and food for everyone. The good years will be followed by seven years of famine when the crops will not grow and the livestock will go hungry.'

"Pharaoh asked Joseph what he thought he should do. Joseph replied that it would be a good idea if someone were put in charge of the food supply for the next seven years and store as much grain as possible – so that when the years of famine came, there would be enough for everyone."

"That's just what I was thinking," said Runt. "I'd have suggested that Pharaoh put me in charge."

Christopher Rabbit smiled. "Joseph didn't need to do that because Pharaoh had already decided to put Joseph in charge. He became the second most important person in Egypt."

"Who was the most important person?" Hector asked.

"Pharaoh, of course," said Runt.

"Is that the end of the story?" asked Whitby.

"No. Remember his brothers?"

"The ones who'd sold him into slavery?" asked Runt.

"Yes. When the years of famine came, people in their land of Canaan suffered too. Their father, Jacob, heard that there was plenty of food in Egypt, and decided to send his ten oldest sons. He gave them money to buy grain. He kept his youngest son, Benjamin, behind."

"Why?" asked Whitby.

"Because he was very fond of him and didn't want any harm to come to him," Christopher Rabbit replied. "The brothers set off. When they arrived in Egypt, they were taken to see Joseph."

"Did they recognize him?" Hector asked.

"No. I expect Joseph looked very different from the little brother they'd got rid of all those years ago."

"He was probably dressed in fine Egyptian clothes," said Caravan Bear.

"Sitting on gorgeous cushions," said Whitby, wriggling on her cushion.

"But did Joseph recognize his brothers?" asked Runt. "That's the real question."

"Yes, he did."

"So did he throw them into prison?" asked Whitby.

"And throw away the key?" Hector added.

"I would have," Runt said firmly. "I'd have treated them as they'd treated me. I think I'd have thrown them into prison first, and then sold them as slaves to a horrible owner who would treat them really badly."

"Joseph didn't do that. Instead he pretended to be angry and called them spies."

"Why did he do that?" asked Caravan Bear.

"Perhaps he wanted to test them to see if they were still dishonest. His brothers protested.

They weren't spies, they said, just brothers who wanted to buy grain. There had been twelve of them, they went on, but one was at home and one had died.

"Joseph pretended not to believe them. He insisted that one of them went to fetch the youngest brother to see if they were telling the truth. The rest would be kept in prison."

"That was an odd thing to say," Hector remarked. "Fetching their youngest brother wouldn't prove they weren't spies."

"Of course he knew they weren't spies!," said Runt. "Haven't you been listening? He wanted to test them."

"I think he also wanted to see if they had changed," Christopher Rabbit said thoughtfully. "He put them all in prison for three days. While they were there, they talked among themselves.

"'We're being punished because of what we did to Joseph,' one of them said.

"'We saw how upset he was when he pleaded for his life, but we wouldn't listen,' said another. They didn't realize that what they were saying was being reported back to Joseph.

"After three days, they were taken out of prison. Joseph insisted on keeping one of the brothers, Simeon, as hostage, then gave orders for their sacks to be filled with grain. He gave them food for the journey but he also ordered his servants to put the silver they had brought to pay for the grain in the sacks."

"Why?" Whitby asked.

"Well, they were his brothers. He probably thought it wouldn't be right to charge them," Hector supposed.

"Bad idea," Runt said. "You should never give favours. That just shows you're weak."

Christopher Rabbit continued. "The brothers loaded the sacks onto their donkeys and left. But when they stopped for the night and found the silver, they were frightened. They arrived home and told their father what had happened. Jacob was very upset at the idea of letting his youngest son, Benjamin, return with them to Egypt and refused permission. So they all remained at home."

"What about poor old Simeon?" asked Whitby.

"Who's Simeon?" Hector asked.

"He was left behind in Egypt as hostage," Whitby explained patiently. "Honestly, Hector, keep up with the story!"

Hector grinned.

"When the grain they'd brought back from Egypt had run out, Jacob told his sons that they would have to return to Egypt to buy more. He agreed, reluctantly, to let Benjamin go with them. He told his sons to take gifts and double the amount of silver.

"When they arrived back they presented the gifts and the silver, and Joseph released Simeon and invited them all to a feast. While they were eating and drinking, Joseph told his steward to fill the brothers' sacks with as much food as they could carry and replace the money that they had brought. He also told him to put his own silver cup in the sack Benjamin was going to carry.

"The next day, the brothers set off for home. When they were on their way, Joseph sent his steward after them to accuse them of stealing the cup."

"Seems a very unkind game to play on his brothers, frightening them like that," Hector said disapprovingly.

"Well, just remember that those same brothers did more than frighten

Joseph when he was younger. They tore off his clothes, threw him into a pit, and then sold him as a slave."

"So that was Joseph's way of getting his own back, was it?" Runt asked.

Christopher Rabbit thought about it. "I don't think it was. I think he wanted to find out if they really were sorry for what they had done to him – and when he found that they were willing to protect their younger brother, Benjamin, and stand in his place, he could see that they had changed."

"Did Joseph tell them who he was?" asked Caravan Bear.

"Yes. When the brothers were brought back to his palace, he threw his arms around them and burst into tears as he told them who he was."

"I bet they were relieved," Whitby said.

"No, they were terrified."

"Why?"

"I imagine they thought it was another trick. Joseph had to convince them that he really was their brother. He told them not to be upset and not to blame themselves for selling him. Joseph was now sure that it was God's will that he had come to Egypt in order to save many lives during the famine.

"He told his brothers to go home and fetch his father and all his brothers' families – and he would give them land so that they would all live near to him. And that's what they did."

Christopher Rabbit closed the Bible.

"So it all ended happily," said Runt. He sounded a bit disappointed.

"Yes. It ended happily."

"I still think Joseph should have had his brothers killed rather than playing games with them and then forgiving them. That's what I'd have done."

"Would you? Why?"

Runt thought for a moment. "To show that I'm in charge. To show I'm not weak. I've never forgiven my brothers and sisters for bullying me when I was little."

"I think Joseph was right," Hector said firmly. "He gave his brothers a taste of what he'd been through and he made them think what it must have been like. Once they had done that, he could see that they were sorry and no longer dishonest."

"Perhaps *then* he felt he could forgive them," said Caravan Bear slowly. "I'm not sure you can forgive someone if they're not sorry."

"God wants us to try, though, doesn't he?" said Christopher Rabbit. "Even if it's hard."

Runt stirred uncomfortably but didn't say anything.

"It's a good story," Caravan Bear said. "It's all about families, quarrels, and making up."

"I think it's all of that and more," said Christopher Rabbit thoughtfully. "I think it's about God turning bad situations into good. And because Joseph trusted in God, God was able to turn the bad situation of Joseph being sold into slavery into something really good – Joseph interpreting Pharaoh's dreams and so saving all Egypt from famine."

Runt stirred. "I've got to go," he said. "I'm a very busy pig. I'm glad it all ended well but I'm not sure about all this forgiveness stuff. If someone behaves badly to me, I can't forgive them. That's just me and it's not done me any harm."

And without a goodbye, he put on his helmet and was off out of the caravan. There was a roar of the motorbike and a flurry of dust.

"Poor Runt," said Christopher Rabbit.

"Oh, I wouldn't say that," said Whitby. "He's happy enough bossing everyone around."

"Perhaps," Christopher Rabbit said doubtfully. "But I expect if he were a kinder pig, he would be much happier – and so would all the pigs at the farm. Please help him, God. And please help us when we need to forgive someone who's hurt us."

6

The Donkey and the Angel

It was high summer when the caravan arrived at the seaside. The sun was shining, the sea was sparkling, and the beach and town were crowded with people on holiday enjoying themselves. Caravan Bear and Hector drove round and round trying to find somewhere to park.

"Look," said Whitby, "there's a funfair over there with a lot of caravans parked behind it."

"They probably belong to the people running the fairground," said Caravan Bear.

"Perhaps we can squeeze in with them," Christopher Rabbit suggested.

The fair was on a patch of grass beside sand dunes leading down to the beach. Caravan Bear guided Hector though the stalls and rides while Whitby gazed around, big-eyed.

"There's a coconut shy! I'd love to have a go at it – I think I'd be able to knock *all* the coconuts off their stands," she said excitedly. "There's a merry-go-round! And do you see that fortune teller's tent over there? Do you think I could get my fortune told?"

"Why do you want your fortune told?" asked Hector.

"I don't know. I'd like to know if something exciting is going to happen."

"The only exciting thing that'll happen is a ball game on the beach after supper," said Caravan Bear. "And perhaps a story, if Christopher Rabbit will read one."

Christopher Rabbit had been looking around the fair with as much wonder as Whitby. "Of course I will," he said, "but can we look around the fair first?"

And that is what they did – after they'd parked the caravan and had their supper. They were only just in time as the funfair had begun packing up and would soon be gone.

Whitby won a plastic duck, and then she and Christopher Rabbit both tried, and failed, to win a coconut. Caravan Bear won a stuffed pink elephant that was almost as large as him.

"Better put it in the caravan before Hector sees it," murmured Christopher Rabbit.

"… or he'll complain about having to carry more stuff," Whitby added.

Hector, meanwhile, had wandered onto the beach and was talking to three donkeys who were giving rides to a crowd of children.

"I offered to help as the donkeys looked tired, but the owner shouted at me to go away," Hector told the others when he went back to the caravan. "I didn't like him. He reminded me of my old master."

After supper, the animals settled down for a story.

"What story are you going to tell us?" Whitby asked.

Christopher Rabbit opened his Bible. "Here's a good one about a donkey," he said.

The animals settled down.

"There once was a man named Balaam. He was a fortune teller…"

"Like the one at the fair?" asked Whitby.

"Perhaps, although Balaam didn't only tell fortunes. He was famous throughout the region for giving prophecies. He was something of a magician and gave blessings and curses."

"What do you mean?" Hector asked.

Christopher Rabbit thought for a minute. "Let's say you wanted to put a curse on your old master. You'd go to Balaam and pay him to curse your old master so that he'd fall ill or die."

"That's an idea," Hector said, his eyes lighting up.

"Did the curses work?" asked Whitby.

Christopher Rabbit shrugged. "I don't know. I suppose so – otherwise he wouldn't have been famous."

"Pretty scary person," Whitby commented.

"Pretty rich person," Caravan Bear added. "I bet he was paid a lot – not just by the people who wanted him to curse someone, but also by the people who didn't want to be cursed."

"Well, he was obviously good at what he did, because when the king of the Moabites, King Balak, wanted a curse put on God's people, the Israelites, he thought of Balaam," Christopher Rabbit went on.

"Why did the king want to put a curse on the Israelites?" asked Hector.

"Because he was scared. He thought that when they arrived and settled on land next to him, they'd take all the best land and food."

"Was this after they'd been wandering around the desert for forty years?" Caravan Bear asked.

"Yes. King Balak got together with the leaders of a neighbouring people, the Midianites, and they agreed to send a group of officials to Balaam. They sent these officials off with a lot of money and a message asking Balaam to return with them and put a curse on the Israelites. 'I know that whoever you bless is blessed and whoever you curse is cursed,' said the message sent by the king.

"It was a long journey. About four hundred miles. When the officials arrived at Balaam's house, he invited them to stay the night. He said he would only go with them if God, the Lord, told him to do so."

"Wise man," Hector nodded.

"That night, God came to Balaam – possibly in a dream – and asked him what the officials wanted."

"Surely God would know what they wanted," Caravan Bear objected, "because God knows everything."

"Do you think he was testing Balaam?" Whitby asked.

"Maybe. Anyway, Balaam explained about King Balak and the curse he was asked to put on the Israelites. God forbade him to go with the officials. He told him not to curse the Israelites because he, God, had already blessed them. They were his people. In the morning, Balaam explained to the officials that God had refused him permission to go with them."

"Did he keep the money?" Whitby asked.

"It doesn't say," said Christopher Rabbit. "When the officials returned to the king with Balaam's message, he sent yet more officials, very important ones, back to Balaam to try to get him to change his mind."

"Did they bring more money?"

"Quite possibly. If he cursed the Israelites, King Balak said, he would pay him well and give him anything he wanted. Balaam asked this group to stay the night while he listened once more to God."

"Why?" asked Hector "God had said no, hadn't he?"

"Perhaps Balaam hoped God would change his mind."

"No, Balaam might have been flattered by the king's offer," Whitby commented.

"God again came to Balaam that night," Christopher Rabbit continued. "He told him to go with the officials, but make sure he did exactly what God told him."

"When do the donkeys come into the story?" Hector asked.

"Just one donkey. Soon."

"Do you think Balaam liked all these important people coming to see him with lots of money and promises of more?" Whitby asked.

Caravan Bear nodded. "It must have been very tempting."

"I'd have been tempted," said Whitby, "if they'd offered me a new ball to play with and perhaps a nice warm coat for the winter."

"I don't expect Balaam had time to play games and he probably had plenty of warm clothes," said Hector.

"Well, the next morning Balaam saddled his donkey and set off with his servants and the officials from the king. As they were riding along, the donkey suddenly saw an angel sent from God with a sword in his hand. So the donkey turned off the road and went into a field."

"Just what I'd do if I saw an angel with a sword," said Whitby.

"And me," said Hector.

"Balaam, who hadn't seen the angel, was angry. He beat the poor donkey and forced her back onto the road. They went on. When they were passing through some vineyards that had tall walls on either side, the donkey again saw the angel standing in front of them. As the donkey couldn't turn off the road, she tried to squeeze past the angel, pressing herself against one of the walls and crushing Balaam's foot."

"Was the donkey beaten again?" Hector asked.

"Yes. He beat the donkey and then they rode on."

"Had the angel disappeared?" asked Whitby.

"He must have or they wouldn't have been able to carry on," Hector observed. "Go on, Christopher Rabbit. What happened next?"

"They reached a very narrow part of the road. The angel appeared once more. This time there was nowhere to turn off so the donkey knelt down. Balaam was furious and beat the donkey with his staff."

"Did she kick him?" asked Hector.

"No. In that moment, God gave her the power to speak. So she said to Balaam, 'Why have you beaten me three times?'

" 'Because you made me look stupid!' Balaam replied angrily."

"I expect the important officials were laughing at him for not being able to control his donkey," Caravan Bear said.

"Perhaps they thought Balaam couldn't ride her," Hector added, "despite him being able to do all those wonderful things like telling fortunes and laying curses here, there, and everywhere."

"It wouldn't have done Balaam's image as a great prophet and magician any good at all," Whitby said.

" 'If I had a sword, I'd kill you!' Balaam went on furiously.

" 'Why?' asked the donkey. 'You've owned me for years and I've never behaved like this before, have I?'

" 'No,' Balaam admitted. And at that moment Balaam saw the angel, standing in the road, a drawn sword in his hand. Balaam fell flat on his face.

" 'Why have you beaten your donkey three times?' the angel asked. 'God sent me to stop you, and if it hadn't been for your donkey, I would have killed you.' "

"Did Balaam turn around and go home?" asked Caravan Bear.

"No. The angel told him to go to King Balak but only tell him what God had said – that God

had blessed the Israelites so that they could not be cursed. And that is exactly what Balaam did. Three times King Balak told Balaam to curse the Israelites. And three times Balaam blessed them instead."

"Why do you think God sent the angel?" Hector asked.

"Do you think that by making Balaam look stupid in front of the officials, God wanted to show Balaam that *he* was in charge, not Balaam?" asked Caravan Bear.

"Perhaps God was testing him, to make sure Balaam wasn't tempted to give in to the king," Christopher Rabbit suggested thoughtfully.

"What happened when Balaam blessed, instead of cursed, the Israelites?" asked Caravan Bear.

"King Balak was very angry. He sent Balaam home without any reward."

Christopher Rabbit closed the Bible.

"Good for Balaam," said Whitby. "It couldn't have been easy refusing to do what the king wanted. I bet I wouldn't have been able to."

"Not if it meant going without presents," Hector teased.

"Balaam might have been tempted to give in to the king if God hadn't sent the angel," Caravan Bear said.

"If you think about it, Balaam *had* been tempted and God would have known – because he knows what we are thinking. That was why he sent the angel, and that was why Balaam couldn't see the angel to begin with," Hector suggested.

"The donkey knew God better than her master did," Christopher Rabbit agreed.

"Good for the donkey," said Hector.

When they woke the next morning, there was no sign of the funfair. There was just a patch of flattened grass. Standing dejectedly in the middle was a donkey.

Hector went over to her. "Shouldn't you have gone with the others?"

"My master didn't want me," the donkey said miserably. "I can't see as well as I used to and he said I couldn't give rides any more – and he didn't see why he should carry on feeding me. So he left me behind."

"That's dreadful."

"Do you know where the fair's gone?" Caravan Bear asked, coming to join them.

"The next town, but it's no good my following. He'd only beat me if I turned up."

The donkey sniffed, and two large tears rolled down her cheeks.

"What's your name?" Hector asked.

"Miranda," the donkey replied. "What am I going to do?"

"Come and have some breakfast," Caravan Bear offered. "We'll work something out."

While they were eating, Christopher Rabbit had an idea.

"I'm sure I saw a sign about donkeys when we were coming into town," he said, "but I can't remember what it was."

"Yes, you did," Whitby said excitedly. "I saw it too. It said 'Donkey Sanctuary'."

"What's that?" asked Miranda.

"It's a home for donkeys like you," said Caravan Bear. "Ones who've been badly treated. You'll be safe there."

After breakfast they set off for the donkey sanctuary, Hector pulling the caravan, and Whitby, Caravan Bear, and Christopher Rabbit sitting on the top step with the donkey trotting alongside. They were given a warm welcome at the sanctuary and Miranda waved goodbye as the caravan set off up the road.

"Please come back and see me," she called. "Thank you!"

"I hope we don't meet any angels, with or without drawn swords," said Whitby as they journeyed on.

"Oh, I don't know," said Hector. "I'd like to meet an angel. I'd take care to stop, though."

"It was a good story," said Caravan Bear.

"Thank you, God, for reminding us how important animals are to you. Please help humans treat us kindly," said Hector.

"And please help us, God, to be strong when we are tempted, so that we do what you tell us," said Christopher Rabbit.

"And thank you, Christopher Rabbit, for reading the story," Whitby finished.

"It was a pleasure," said Christopher Rabbit.

Jacob and Esau

Christopher Rabbit finished stirring the pot of food that was suspended over a small bonfire outside the caravan. He sniffed. Mmm, that smelled good. He licked the spoon. Mmm, it tasted even better.

"You shouldn't do that," came a disapproving voice from behind him.

Christopher Rabbit turned to find two small pigs staring at him.

"Mother says it's dirty to lick spoons," said one of the pigs.

"Not that we take any notice of what she says," said the other pig. "Can we have a lick?"

"No," said Christopher Rabbit. "It's for our supper."

The first pig grabbed the spoon, stuck it into the pot, and then licked it noisily. "Tastes good," she said.

"Me, me!" squealed the second pig.

"There's not enough for you as well," the first pig retorted, and she had another dip into the pot and another lick of the spoon.

"Stop that!" said Christopher Rabbit in a firm voice. "Who are you?"

"I'm May and that's Maytwo," said the first pig, putting the spoon back into the pot and scooping out some more of the stew.

"Horrid names, aren't they?" said Maytwo. "Especially mine. Dad's idea..."

"... of course!" said May, pulling a face. "He always has the daftest ideas."

"We're twins," Maytwo explained. "And as they weren't expecting two of us, they hadn't thought of a second name. So I got stuck with this stupid one."

"Better than Dad's name," said May. "Whoever calls a pig 'Runt'?"

"Bit of a pain really, having a dad called after the smallest of the litter," Maytwo explained.

"Bit of a pain having a dad like Dad," May added.

"EMBARRASSING!" they shouted together and squealed with laughter.

"Dad said we'd find you here."

Maytwo stared hard at Christopher Rabbit. "I bet you're Christopher Rabbit," she said. "Did you know I can pull horrid faces?"

She did so.

"So can I." Her sister pulled an even more horrid face.

To Christopher Rabbit's relief, he saw Caravan Bear, Whitby, and Hector approach. They'd gone shopping while Christopher Rabbit had stayed behind to cook supper.

"This is May and this is Maytwo," he told them. "They're Runt's children."

"Only two of them," May corrected. "There are eleven more."

"But we're the oldest," Maytwo smirked.

"*I'm* the oldest," said May firmly.

"And I'm the cleverest," Maytwo added. "Just like Dad."

"EMBARRASSING!" May shouted, and they both squealed with laughter.

"We've come for a story," May said. "But we don't mind if you have your supper first. We'll help you eat it."

"Just like their dad," Whitby murmured under her breath.

As they finished eating, they heard the roar of a motorbike. It was Runt.

"I see you've met my little angels!" he called as he dismounted.

"Trouble," May said.

"Big trouble," Maytwo added.

"Aren't they darlings?" said Runt, beaming with pride.

May and Maytwo looked at each other. "Embarrassing!" they said and laughed.

As it was a warm night, everyone settled down outside the caravan and Christopher Rabbit fetched his Bible.

"If it's boring, we'll take ourselves off," May declared.

"We didn't really want to come but Dad said we should," Maytwo said. "Not that we listen to him, but we didn't have anything better to do," she added.

"Now, girls." Runt smiled fondly.

Christopher Rabbit opened his Bible.

"I think you'll like this story," he said. "It's about twins. Their names were Jacob and Esau."

"Esau sounds like seesaw," said May.

Christopher Rabbit sighed. It was going to be a difficult evening.

"Esau had been born first but Jacob came almost immediately after him. When they were born, Jacob was holding on to Esau's heel."

"Why?" asked Maytwo.

"I don't know."

"Perhaps you held on to my tail when we were born," May commented. "As I was born first."

"But I'm the cleverer one," Maytwo said smugly.

May pushed her.

"Esau grew up to be bigger and stronger than his brother," Christopher Rabbit continued quickly. "He was a big man and had thick hair all over his body."

"I've got thick hair all over my body," Hector said complacently. "But I don't boast about it."

"I don't think Esau boasted about it," Christopher Rabbit said. "It was just how he was. Jacob wasn't at all like him. He didn't look like him and they weren't alike in other ways. Esau liked the outdoor life while Jacob was happy staying at home with his mother."

"I bet she loved him the best," Hector remarked.

"Just like my parents loved *me* the best," said Runt.

"And you love *us* the best," said Maytwo.

"Although you love me the bestest of all because I'm the oldest," May added in a superior voice.

"But I'm the cleverest." Maytwo smiled sweetly.

"No, you're not!"

"Yes, I am!"

Runt beamed. "See how bright they are?"

Christopher Rabbit hurried on. "One day Jacob was home cooking some stew when Esau arrived. 'Let me have some of that – I'm starving!' he demanded.

"Jacob replied, 'You can have some, but only if you give me all the rights that you have as the firstborn son.'"

"Sounds as if he was jealous of his brother," Whitby commented.

"I don't think he liked being born second," Caravan Bear remarked.

"Well, how would *you* like it?" Maytwo asked.

"I don't think I'd mind," Caravan Bear said after some thought.

"That's only because you don't know what it's like," Maytwo retorted.

"Perhaps that's why Jacob held on to Esau's heel when he was born. He was trying to push him out of the way," Hector suggested.

"Perhaps," said Christopher Rabbit. "Anyway, Esau was so hungry that he agreed. He didn't think much of the firstborn rights anyway. 'Not much use being the firstborn if I die from hunger,' he said.

"'Promise?' Jacob asked.

"'I promise,' Esau replied, and he gobbled up all the stew."

"What were the rights of the firstborn son?" Maytwo asked.

"Would it have meant becoming the head of the family after their father died?" Caravan Bear asked.

"I think so," Christopher Rabbit agreed.

"Well, I think that was a pretty stupid thing for Esau to do," Caravan Bear said. "Giving up all the rights of being head of the family just for a meal."

"But if he was hungry…?" Whitby suggested.

"Even so," Caravan Bear said firmly.

"Their father, Isaac, was old," Christopher Rabbit went on. "He'd gone blind and knew he didn't have long to live. He called Esau to him. 'You are my firstborn and I want you to do something for me. Go and hunt a wild animal and

then cook it the way I like. When I've eaten it, I will give you my blessing before I die.' Esau's and Jacob's mother, Rebekah, was in the room when he said this."

"I thought Esau had already traded off giving up his firstborn rights to Jacob in return for a plate of stew," Hector said.

"He had, but he'd probably forgotten all about it. And, of course, his father, Isaac, didn't know what he'd done.

"Anyway, Esau went off to do what his father had asked," Christopher Rabbit continued. His mother, though, wasn't happy about this. She felt that Jacob should receive the special blessing even though he hadn't been born first."

"I said she loved him the best," said Hector complacently.

"So instead of leaving it to God to work out his plan for her sons, she plotted how to trick her husband," Christopher Rabbit continued.

"Why did she do that?" May asked.

"Perhaps she thought Jacob would make a better head of the family than Esau?" suggested Caravan Bear. "And she might have thought that Esau was only getting what he deserved when he gave up his birthright for a meal."

"Especially a meal of stew," said Hector, wrinkling up his nose. "Give me a good bag of oats any day."

"Maybe she thought that if Jacob was head of the family he'd listen to her, so she'd really be the one in charge," Runt said cynically.

"She probably just loved Jacob best. Parents often have favourites although they won't admit it," said Hector.

"I love all my children equally," Runt declared.

"Oh, Dad, you know that's not true!" May replied. "You love us best and me best of all!"

"That's not fair!" shouted Maytwo.

"Now, girls, sit down and behave!" Runt said. "Lots of spirit," he said to the others. "Just like me when I was their age!"

May and Maytwo looked at each other.

"He's so…" May began.

"… embarrassing!" Maytwo finished.

"Shall I get on with the story?" Christopher Rabbit asked. "The really good bit is to come."

"I want to know what Rebekah's plan was," said Whitby.

" 'Go and kill two tasty young goats,' she told Jacob. 'I'll cook them into a delicious stew. You give it to your father and he'll give you his blessing.' "

"Wouldn't he know he was blessing the wrong son?" asked Runt.

"That's what Jacob said. 'What if Dad touches me?' he asked. 'He'd know straight away that I am not Esau as I'm not hairy like him.' Rebekah had planned for that. When Jacob returned with the goats, she dressed him in Esau's clothes."

"Why?" Maytwo demanded.

"Because they smelled of the outdoors. Then she covered his hands and his neck with goatskins so that when Isaac touched him, he would think it was his oldest son, the hairy Esau."

"That's not a nice thing to do," said Whitby.

"Oh, I don't know," Runt disagreed. "I think it's a clever plan."

"But it was tricking an old, blind man," Whitby protested.

"Why didn't God stop them?" asked Caravan Bear.

"I don't think God works like that," Christopher Rabbit said. "God gave us the freedom to choose what we do. We can choose to do good things or bad things. But God's always there to pick up the pieces."

"Did their plot work?" asked May.

"Oh yes, although Isaac was a bit suspicious at first. 'You have the voice of Jacob but you smell like

Esau.' He touched Jacob's hand and felt the hairy goatskin. 'Are you really my son, Esau?' he asked.

"'I am,' Jacob replied. Isaac ate the food Jacob had prepared and then gave him the blessing given to the firstborn. But as soon as Jacob had left the room, Esau came running in. He'd caught some venison, made a stew, and was bringing it to his father."

"All this talk of food is making me hungry," remarked Whitby.

"You've had plenty to eat," said Caravan Bear. "Go on, Christopher Rabbit. I want to hear what happened."

"Esau said, 'Please sit up and eat this lovely meal I've made for you, Dad. Then you can give me your blessing.'"

"I bet that confused his father," Hector commented.

"It did. 'Who are you?' Isaac asked.

"'I'm your son, Esau. Your firstborn.'

"Isaac started to tremble. 'Then who came just before you did? I ate the food and gave the person who brought it my blessing.'

"Esau realized he'd been tricked for the second time. 'Jacob took my birthright and now he's taken the blessing that should have been given to me,' he shouted."

"Couldn't his father bless him as well?" asked Caravan Bear.

"No. Once it had been given, the blessing couldn't be changed. When Isaac died, Jacob would be in charge of everything and everyone in the family and that included Esau."

"I bet he was angry," said Hector.

"He was furious. He vowed he would kill his brother."

"And did he?" asked May.

"No. When their mother heard what Esau threatened, she sent Jacob away to live with relatives."

Everyone was quiet for a moment.

"Was Jacob sorry for what he'd done?" asked Whitby.

"I think so," said Christopher Rabbit. "He'd schemed against his brother. He'd broken his father's heart. His brother had sworn to kill him, and his mother, who planned it all, was telling him to run away. I think he was sorry and ashamed. So off he went.

"When it grew dark, he lay down on the ground to try and sleep. He put a stone under his head to act as a pillow."

"Pity he didn't have a caravan," said Hector.

"While he slept, he dreamed he saw a staircase that rested on the earth and reached up to heaven. Bright angels climbed up and down. Then, in his dream, he saw God, who told him not to be frightened. God

told him that he would give him and his descendants the land he was lying on. He said he would look after him wherever he went and would bring him safely home one day."

"Was that the same Jacob who was the father of Joseph in the other stories you told us?" Runt asked suddenly.

"That's right. He became the father of the twelve tribes of Israel."

"So why did God look after him after the way he'd behaved?" Runt demanded.

"I think God looks after everyone, no matter how badly they behave," said Caravan Bear.

"I think that's true," Christopher Rabbit agreed. "God would have known that Jacob was truly sorry about what he'd done and learned some lessons."

"And of course God would know that because Jacob was sorry, he would be given the land – because God knows everything that happens," Caravan Bear added.

"Time we went home," said Runt, stretching himself. He turned to his daughters. "Did you like that story?"

May shrugged. "All right, I suppose." She glanced at her sister. "Don't you try any tricks like that on me," she said threateningly.

Maytwo pulled a face. "If I did, you wouldn't know anything about it," she said, "because I'm twice as clever as you."

Runt laughed. "What did I tell you? Sharp as anything. But not as sharp as their father!"

"Oh, Dad!" said May.

"Can't take him anywhere," Maytwo added.

"EMBARRASSING!" they shouted together and wandered off, laughing.

Once they'd gone and Runt had roared off on his motorbike, Christopher Rabbit, Caravan Bear, and Whitby looked at each other.

"Well…" Whitby began.

"Well…" Caravan Bear went on.

"Absolutely," Hector finished.

"I'm glad that's over," Christopher Rabbit said thankfully.

"Embarrassing," grinned Whitby.

"Let's hope God can sort them out," Caravan Bear said.

"I'm sure he will," Christopher Rabbit replied, and they went into the caravan and were soon asleep.

8

Esther, the Queen

The leaves were turning brown and fluttering from the trees as Christopher Rabbit, Caravan Bear, and Whitby walked beside Hector along the road leading to Christopher Rabbit's home. The sun was shining but a keen wind was blowing, and they walked at a brisk pace in order to keep warm.

They didn't speak as they walked, each animal deep in thought.

"Autumn," thought Hector, sniffing the air. "It's been a good holiday but I'll be glad to get home and have a rest in my comfortable stable without having to tow a heavy caravan."

"Autumn," thought Caravan Bear. "It'll be good to be home for a while." He glanced back at the caravan.

"Needs a thorough clean inside and out, and I might do some painting." He smiled happily. Caravan Bear liked painting.

"Autumn," thought Whitby. "It'll be sad not to have any adventures for a while but I can tell all my friends about everything we've seen and done – and it'll be good to curl up on the hearthrug in front of the fire."

"Autumn," thought Christopher Rabbit. "In a way, I suppose it will be nice to be home, but it's been such a lovely summer with Caravan Bear, Whitby, and Hector. I'll miss them." He heaved a sigh.

As they turned into the road leading to Christopher Rabbit's burrow, a familiar figure came running to meet them. It was Min the cat, who lived next door to Christopher Rabbit. Normally calm and placid and very much in charge, Min looked upset.

"I'm so glad you've come!" she cried.

"Whatever's the matter?" asked Christopher Rabbit.

"Weasels! Three of them!"

Christopher Rabbit looked past Min into his front garden. "What's my best rocking chair and some of my other furniture doing on the lawn?" he asked, mystified.

"Oh dear. It's so complicated!"

"Why don't we go inside and you can explain?" Caravan Bear suggested as the caravan came to a stop outside Christopher Rabbit's front gate.

Min turned to him. "That's just it. That's the problem. They're in there and I don't know what to do about them."

"Who are in where?"

"The weasels, of course. I've been trying to tell you!" She turned to Christopher Rabbit. "I heard this dreadful noise coming from your burrow so I ran straight around. I didn't even stop to put down my knitting."

Min loved knitting and gave her whole family woolly clothes that they only wore when they came to visit her.

"The door was open," she went on, "and when I went in, there was the most awful noise. The weasels, you know, the ones that have been breaking into animals' homes for the past few months – only of course you wouldn't know because you've been away – well, there they were, sitting at your table, drinking your elderflower wine and singing at the tops of their voices. And the mess the room was in! I think they'd been having a party."

"So what did you do?" asked Christopher Rabbit in a small voice.

"I didn't know what to do so I just hissed at them and spat. They jumped up and rushed toward me and I threw my knitting straight at them. It wasn't much of a weapon but it was all I had. The weasels skidded on the knitting needles, and the ball of wool unwound and tangled itself around their legs. They fell over each other and I think they must have knocked themselves out because they didn't get up."

"Are they still there?"

"I don't know. I just came running out."

The animals looked at one another.

"We'd better arm ourselves," said Caravan Bear. He disappeared inside the caravan and returned with a frying pan.

"We don't need weapons," Hector snorted. "We're more than a match for three drunken weasels! Come on."

With that, he charged up the path and everyone followed. Once inside they stopped and listened, but all was quiet. They went into Christopher Rabbit's living room.

The weasels had gone.

"They must have left by the back door," Min said.

They looked around. The room was in a terrible mess. There were upturned chairs and smashed glasses. Broken crockery littered the floor and the remains of food were everywhere, ground into the carpet and spattered up the walls. A trail of elderflower wine spread across Christopher Rabbit's highly polished table and dripped onto the floor.

Christopher Rabbit gulped and closed his eyes. The smashed crockery had been his best china tea set, given to him by his great-aunt Hettie.

"I'm very sorry," Min said, touching his paw.

"Is everywhere like this?" he asked, fighting back tears.

"I don't know but I expect so. I think they were planning to steal the furniture."

"What they haven't smashed up," Caravan Bear added in a grim voice.

"Shall I go after them?" Hector asked.

"Don't bother," said a voice from the door. It was Henry the beaver. Behind him were his four sons.

"They ran past as we were building a dam. All tangled up in strands of wool they were, falling over their own feet. Made me and my boys laugh to see them!"

"Did you catch them?" Whitby asked eagerly.

"Didn't need to. They weren't looking where they were going and fell straight into the duck pond. That made me and my boys laugh even more. The ducks started pecking them and I've no doubt they will give them a good talking-to. I don't think we'll see them around this way again."

Christopher Rabbit looked around the room and shuddered. It would be a long time before he felt it was his home once more. He sat down on the floor and a tear rolled down his cheek.

"I wish I'd come earlier," said Min sadly. "I'm so very sorry."

Caravan Bear sat down beside Christopher Rabbit. "We'll park the caravan in your garden," he said, "and stay until we've got everything tidied up. I'm very good at painting," he added.

"We'll all help, and so will everyone around here," Henry the beaver said, and his sons murmured agreement. "The boys and I are good at carpentry if you need anything mending."

It was festive in the garden that evening as Caravan Bear, helped by Henry and his sons, strung lights up between the trees. As it grew dark, Susie the squirrel and Frank the mole arrived with their families and Lantwit the owl flew in and perched on a nearby branch of a tree. They all wanted to know what had happened and Christopher Rabbit was overwhelmed with offers of help.

Everyone had brought food and drink with them, and when they had all eaten and drunk, Caravan Bear turned to Christopher Rabbit.

"Do you think you might read us a story?" he asked.

"Oh, I don't know…"

Christopher Rabbit looked at the expectant faces gazing at him.

"All right."

He fetched his Bible from the caravan and settled down on the steps. The animals crowded around him.

"I think," he began, "I'll read the story of Queen Esther, who was something of a star – and I think Min has been something of a star herself."

"Don't be so silly," Min protested.

Christopher Rabbit began to read. "The king of Persia, King Xerxes, was a very rich and very powerful king. Everyone had to obey him. He married a beautiful Jewish girl, Esther. Her older cousin, Mordecai, warned her not to let the king know that she was Jewish."

"Why?" asked Whitby.

"I don't know," Christopher Rabbit said honestly.

"Maybe because they were afraid that the king might turn against them?" suggested Caravan Bear.

"From the other stories you've told us, it seems that the Jews often had a hard time of it in different countries," muttered Hector, busy chewing some oats. He was still hungry, even after a very large meal.

"Perhaps. Anyway, soon after the king and Esther were married, Mordecai discovered that there was a plot to kill the king. He told Esther, who told the king, and the plot came to nothing. But the king commanded that details of the plot – including Mordecai's name – be written in the Book of Records."

Henry nodded wisely. "Good idea to keep records. I've got a little book in which I write down all the streams I've dammed and what's happened to them. You never know when it'll come in useful."

As everyone looked puzzled at this, he explained. "If there's a flood, I might have to undam a stream so water doesn't run into anyone's property."

"I see," said Caravan Bear.

"I do that too," said Frank the mole. "I keep detailed plans, otherwise I'd get lost down all the tunnels I've made."

Christopher Rabbit continued. "Now, the king's highest official was a man called Haman. He hated the Jews and he especially hated Mordecai."

"I expect he saw him as a threat. *He* hadn't found out about the plot to kill the king, had he?" muttered Henry.

"It was more than that. The king had commanded that everyone should bow down to Haman, as his high official. But Mordecai refused, for it was against the religion of the Jews to bow down to anyone other than God."

"I don't blame him," said Min, busily knitting. She had found her knitting needles and started on a fresh ball of wool. "I never heard anything so ridiculous."

"Haman didn't think it ridiculous. When Mordecai refused to bow down to him, he planned to have every Jew in Persia killed. He persuaded the king that on a certain date every single Jew throughout the whole land should die."

"How did Haman persuade the king?" asked Whitby.

"He told the king that the Jews had different laws from the law of the king and therefore they were breaking the king's laws. Haman also said that he would pay a lot of money into the king's treasuries if the king agreed to destroy the Jews."

"With humans, it often comes down to money," said Hector, shaking his head. "Why they can't live without it I'll never know."

"When Mordecai heard about these plans, he sent word to Esther to beg her to try and get the king to change his mind. Esther was frightened. She knew that anyone going to the king without being summoned by him risked being killed – especially if the king didn't want to see them."

"But she was the queen, after all," Min objected.

"The king had power of life and death over all his subjects, including the queen," said Christopher Rabbit.

"And the king didn't know she was Jewish," said Caravan Bear.

"Did she agree to go?" hooted Lantwit.

"Yes. She asked Mordecai and all the Jewish people to pray for her. Then she approached the king."

"And...?" Whitby asked as Christopher Rabbit stopped to take a breath.

"Fortunately the king was pleased to see her. Her excuse for going to the king was to invite him and Haman to a banquet the following day, and they accepted."

"Was she going to kill Haman at the banquet?" asked Whitby.

"No," said Christopher Rabbit. "That wasn't her plan. Haman went home that night very pleased with himself. He boasted to his wife and his friends that the invitation showed just how important he had become. To be invited to a feast given by the queen with the king as the only other guest showed how very powerful he was.

"The only thing to spoil Haman's pleasure that day was when he saw Mordecai. Mordecai was the man who refused to bow down to him. He complained about him to his wife and she suggested that he build a gallows outside the palace gates on which to hang Mordecai. Haman thought this was a fantastic idea. He would have Mordecai hanged – and then go to the banquet. He gave orders for the gallows to be built and then went to bed."

"And slept soundly, I expect," said Min. "Nasty piece of work!"

"That same night, the king couldn't sleep. He ordered that the Book of Records be brought to him. His servant read aloud the section containing the plan to kill the king and Mordecai's part in uncovering the plot.

" 'What reward has been given to that man?' the king asked.

" 'Nothing,' the servant replied.

"Just then Haman entered the court, having come early in order to ask the king's permission to have Mordecai hanged. 'What should be done for the man whom the king wishes to reward?' the king asked Haman."

Lantwit hooted with laughter. "I bet Haman thought the king meant *him*!"

"That's right," Christopher Rabbit replied. "Haman thought that the king wished to reward *him*. So he replied, 'Let him be dressed in some of the king's own robes and given one of the king's own horses as well as a royal crown. Then let this man ride through the streets with a servant leading the way proclaiming that this is the man whom the king wishes to reward.'

" 'Right,' said the king. 'Do all this to Mordecai.' "

All the animals burst out laughing.

"Served him right," said Min.

"Did Haman do it?" asked Susie.

"He had to," Christopher Rabbit replied. "Don't forget that the king was all-powerful. Haman was the one who had to lead Mordecai, who was dressed in the king's fine robes and sitting on the king's fine horse, right through the streets of the city and proclaim that this was the man whom the king wished to reward. Haman was furious but there was nothing he could do about it.

"The next thing that happened was the banquet the queen had prepared. The food was delicious, the wine was the finest, and the king was so pleased at the way he had been entertained that he said to Esther, his queen, 'If there is anything you would like, even half my kingdom, just ask and it will be granted.'

"So she told him of the plot to kill her people. 'What wicked person planned this?' the king asked.

"'Haman,' she replied. The king ordered Haman be hanged on the gallows he had built to hang Mordecai."

"Hold on a minute," objected Hector. "I thought the king agreed to Haman's plan to kill all the Jews. Bit unfair, wasn't it, for him to put all the blame on to Haman? Not that Haman was a very nice person, but fair's fair."

Christopher Rabbit shrugged. "I don't think fairness comes into it if you're a king with all that power."

"I suppose it doesn't," Hector muttered.

"The king then told Esther that he would cancel Haman's order to kill all the Jews, and instead decreed that the Jews could keep their own laws and rights. And he made Mordecai his chief adviser in Haman's place," Christopher Rabbit finished.

A cheer went up from everyone in the garden, apart from Hector.

"I wouldn't have taken that job," he said. "It seems all too easy to upset a king like that."

"I don't suppose the king would have given you the job anyway," said Whitby.

Christopher Rabbit closed his Bible. "And that's the end of the story, except that each year since then Jews have held a festival to celebrate Esther's bravery in risking her life to serve God and save her people."

"Perhaps we should hold a festival to celebrate Min's bravery over the weasels," Caravan Bear said.

"I wasn't brave at all," Min protested.

"We could have a knitting festival," suggested Whitby, and everyone laughed.

"We'll come around tomorrow and help clean up," the animals assured Christopher Rabbit as they prepared to go home.

"Before you all go," Christopher Rabbit said, "I'd just like to thank all of you. I was very sad when I saw what the weasels had done to my home and my nice things, but you've made me realize that friends are worth much more than any furniture or crockery."

The animals were as good as their word. In no time at all Christopher Rabbit's furniture was mended, and the rooms cleaned, painted, and polished. When he finally moved back into the burrow, everything was sparkling and, he had to admit, looked better than it had done before.

On his first night back home, he sat in his new rocking chair in front of a roaring fire and looked around. He remembered how Caravan Bear and Whitby had painted the walls, as well as splattering themselves; how Henry and his sons had mended his furniture; how Lantwit had flown far and wide to find another tea set like the one given to him by his great-aunt Hettie; how Hector had cleared away

everything that had been broken; and how Min, now curled up on a rug that she had knitted herself, had supervised all the work.

"What a fortunate rabbit I am," he said out loud. "Thank you, God. Thank you for the story of Esther, who was so brave, and for Min, who was also brave. And thank you especially for all my good friends."

And next spring, he thought, Caravan Bear, Whitby, and Hector would arrive and they would be off on new adventures – here, there, wherever the fancy took them!

Other titles by
Avril Rowlands

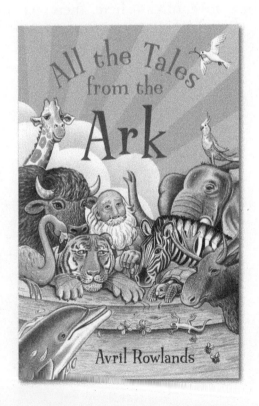

The Animals' Caravan

The Journey Begins

Avril Rowlands

Adventures through the
Bible with Caravan Bear
and friends

The Animals' Caravan

Stories Jesus Told

Avril Rowlands

Adventures through the Bible with
Caravan Bear and friends